Benjamin F. (Benjamin Franklin) Taylor

Songs of Yesterday

Benjamin F. (Benjamin Franklin) Taylor

Songs of Yesterday

ISBN/EAN: 9783337181970

Printed in Europe, USA, Canada, Australia, Japan

Cover: Foto ©Thomas Meinert / pixelio.de

More available books at **www.hansebooks.com**

SONGS OF YESTERDAY.

BY

BENJ. F. TAYLOR,

AUTHOR OF "OLD TIME PICTURES," "THE WORLD ON WHEELS,"
"IN CAMP AND FIELD," ETC.

WITH ILLUSTRATIONS.

CHICAGO:
S. C. GRIGGS AND COMPANY.
1876.

A BANK NOTE.

—————

Hart L. Weaver, Esq.,
   La Porte, Indiana.

> My Dear Sir :
>
> As a Banker, you deal in figures of fact; but I commit no error in cordially inscribing to you this Volume of figures of fancy.
>
> As a little token of regard for a friend in need and in deed, and a man "to count on" everywhere, I am glad to believe you will accept this note without either indorsers or discount, and simply with the signature of
>
> Yours Always and Sincerely,

Benj. F. Taylor

THESE little poems are like Lot's Wife; they all look over their shoulders. Unlike the savory lady who became muriate of soda, they are not looking back upon Sodom but upon Paradise.

As there is a vague rumor of a Wandering Jew, so there is a suspicion of a man somewhere who never had a childhood, but bounded into being full-grown. To be brought to a premature end is bad, but to be brought to a premature beginning is yet worse. For him these glimpses of old days, rudely literal as a Dutch etching upon a tile, can have no charm.

But whoever has an Eden, where a little plat of grass that was never plowed or mown keeps always green; where the mysteries of Christmas Eves and the peopled twilights, and the memories of simpler times yet linger unrebuked;—for him, perhaps, some of these poems may have a certain quaint old flavor and fragrance, as of caraway and dill.

The chief of earthly arts is the art of keeping always young. Time takes heavy toll as we pass, one after one, the Janus-gated years, but he goes bravely through the world who bears with him the perfume of his Eden and the romance of the morning and the lavish heart of youth.

CONTENTS.

Illustrations

SONGS OF YESTERDAY.

MARY BUTLER'S RIDE.

THE story of Mary Butler's Ride is unembellished truth. To one of her grandsons, J. M. Taylor, Esq., of New York, I am indebted for the incident, and to another, the Honorable Arthur M. Eastman, of New Hampshire, for a spray

from the old Blush Rose, set out by Lieutenant Eastman, of the Minute Men, one hundred years ago. It lies upon the table, as I write, a withered but an eloquent witness, as if to perfume the poem with its fragrant testimony.

To hear men say — those far-away boys of hers, and yet busy in life's affairs,—" Many a time I have heard her tell the story!" brings the gray-eyed Mary Butler strangely near. It is like raising a dead century to instant resurrection.

The rhymes and the rose-leaves are a little love-token to the coming Centennial.

MARY BUTLER'S RIDE.

I.

EBENEZER EASTMAN, of Gilmanton, is dead;—
    At least they had him buried full fifty years ago;—
    The gray White Mountain granite they set above his head,
    With some graven words upon it, to let the neighbors know
    Precisely what it was that made the grasses grow
So wondrous rank and strong. How they rippled in the wind,
As if nobody ever died, nobody ever sinned!
To that old Bible name of his what eloquence was lent
When its owner marched to battle,—not a ration, not a tent,
Nor a promise nor a sign of a Continental cent!
Ho, Ebenezer Eastman! We'll call the roll again,—
Ho, dead and gone Lieutenant of the old-time Minute Men!

II.

Plowing land for turnips, with awkward Buck and Bright,
    Was stout Lieutenant Eastman, one lovely day in June;
He "hawed" them to the left and he "geed" them to the right,

And they slowly came about in the lazy summer noon,

    He humming to himself the fragment of a tune,

Which he would croon at night to the baby-boy who lay

In basswood trough becradled first, a week ago that day!

I count the times the Blush Rose bloomed. Exactly ninety-
      eight

Since Eastman's fingers planted it beside the garden gate.

Almost one hundred years ago! I know 'tis rather late

To muster in the furloughed man and make him march again,—

But smell the old Blush Roses! They are just as sweet as then!

III.

All at a flying gallop a rider swings in sight,

    Pulls up beside the fallow and gives the view-halloo,—

His horse's flanks are black, but his neck is foamy white:—

    "Turn out! Lieutenant Eastman! There's something else
      to do!

    The red-coats are a-swarming! Your summer plowing's
      through!"

No other word — away! And the rattling of the hoofs

Was like the rain from traveling clouds along the cabin roofs.

The plowman turned his cattle out; he saddled up the bay,

And he rallied out the wilderness upon that summer day,

And the Minute Men of Gilmanton to Boston marched away.

About the Mother? Well, she watched beside the cabin door,

And rocked the baby's basswood boat upon the puncheon floor.

"PLOWING LAND FOR TURNIPS, WITH AWKWARD BUCK AND BRIGHT."

IV.

Days grew long in Gilmanton, and weeds among the corn;

  The quoiting-ground was grassy, and louder ran the rill;

The wrestling-match was over,—the smithy was forlorn,—

  The spiders in the empty door had swung their webs at will,—

The champions had gone to Bunker's smoky Hill,

To try the quaint, old-fashioned "lock" they practiced on the
    Green,

And such a game of tough "square hold" the world had seldom
    seen!

About the Father? Only this: He fought in Stark's brigade,

On Charlestown Neck, that dusty day. A splendid mark he made:

He never flinched a single inch when British cannon played,

But foddered up an old rail fence with Massachusetts hay,

Stood out the battle at the rack, and stoutly blazed away!

V.

Lo, through the smoky glory, that human Flower-de-luce,

 The gray-eyed Mary Butler, Lieutenant Eastman's wife!

Her pallid cheek and brow like a holy flag of truce,

 Her heart as sweet and red as a rose's inner life,

 No murmur on her lips, nor sign of any strife.

Four days before the fight. Has the little woman heard

From anybody Boston way? Nobody — not a word!

The maple woods, that round her stand so solemn in the calm,

Up and down are swaying slowly, like a singing-master's palm,

All together beating time, — not a soul to sing a psalm!

"There's been a dreadful battle!" — that's what the neighbor said,

"But when or where I cannot tell, nor who is hurt or dead."

VI.

Then up rose Mary Butler, and set her wheel at rest;

She swept the puncheon floor, she washed the cottage pride,—

The cottage pride of three weeks old, and dressed him in his
best,—

" THE QUOITING-GROUND WAS GRASSY."

She wound the clock that told the time her mother was a
bride,

And porringer and spoon she deftly laid aside;

She strung a clean white apron across the window panes,

And swung the kettle from the crane, for fear of rusting rains;

Then tossed the saddle on the bay and donned her linen gown,

And took the baby on before,—no looking round or down!

Full seventy miles to Cambridge town! Bring out your civic
      crown!

I think 'twill fit that brow of hers who sadly smiled and said:

"We'll *know* about your father, boy, and who is hurt or dead!"

VII.

Rugged maples broke their ranks to let the rider by,

      Fell in behind her noiseless as falls the stealthy dew;

Such heavy folds of starless dark in double shadow lie,

      The slender bridle-path she threads can only just show
            through,

      And buried in the leafy miles was all the world she knew.

By muffled drum of partridge and jaunty jay-bird's fife,

That mother made her lonely march,—that Continental wife.

She never drew the bridle-rein till forty miles were done,

And on her ended journey shone the second setting sun,

And round the Bay, like battle-clock, tolled out the evening gun.

Talk not of pomps and tournaments! If you had only seen

The royal ride from Gilmanton, the halt at Cambridge Green!

VIII.

Dust-bedimmed and weary, with a look as if she smiled,

  She melted through the haze of the summer's smoky gold!

Some Master's faded picture of Madonna and the Child,

"SHE NEVER DREW THE BRIDLE-REIN TILL FORTY MILES WERE DONE."

Born full a thousand years ago, and never growing old!

  She heard old Putnam's kennel growl, the bells of Charles-

    town tolled;

She saw the golden day turn gray within an ashen shroud,

That showed the scarlet Regulars like lightning through a cloud

Forth from the furnace and the fire Lieutenant Eastman came,—
The smell of powder in his clothes and fragrance in his fame,—
And met her bravely waiting there, who bore his boy and
    name!—
She from the howling wilderness — he from the hell of men.
The little woman called the roll: he called it back again!

IX.

Then lightly to the pillion the gray-eyed wife he swung,
    A bundle on the saddle-bow all tenderly he placed,
And, lost amid the leafy calms where cannon never rung,
    Away they rode to Gilmanton, her arm around his waist.
    No general's sash of crimson silk so rarely could have
        graced!
Ah, Mary Butler cannot die, whatever sextons say,
While yet her azure pulses keep their old heroic play.
That splendid nerve of hers was strung like Morse's filmy
    bridge
To hearts that beat at Gettysburg, Arkansas' dismal ridge.
To Captain bold of cavalry, her grandchild's gallant son;
To Sergeant of the Boys in Blue who wears the scars he won.
Her dauntless soul electric,—a spark of fire divine,—
Was flashed like thought by telegraph, along the slender line!
The thing she was on Bunker's day an Angel might have been,

The song-bird to the wounded troops, the Nightingale to men,
And on that later Flodden field lived Clara once again.

A million men have lingered long, a million men have died,
Who never saw a deed so grand as MARY BUTLER'S RIDE!

"AWAY THEY RODE TO GILMANTON, HER ARM AROUND HIS WAIST."

KELLY'S FERRY.

—

THE flowers of battle are not always crimson. Some of them are white as snow. During the late war, Kelly's Ferry, on the Tennessee, was a scene of mingled men, mud, profanity and mules, and as desolate as Hogarth's "End of All Things;" but no fairer flower ever blossomed anywhere than when the Third Ohio Blues fed the fainting Fifty-fourth Virginia Grays, captured at the Storming of Mission Ridge. The flower is called Fraternity, and they had brought it all the way from Georgia, where those same Grays were hosts, those very Blues the famished guests, and set it out beside the lazy Tennessee. It was the writer's fortune to see one of the grandest battles of all the war, when "Greek met Greek" in a gallantry so splendid that it lights up that far November day as with the glory of an Easter sun; but never anything so fine as that.

Those two banquets make a pair of pictures never to be turned to the wall. And the flower, Fraternity, that, drenched with costly blood, yet lived—let it be transplanted from Kelly's Ferry far and near, till it blossoms in all weathers and beautifies the whole land.

KELLY'S FERRY.

I.

HAVE you read in any book, heard anybody tell
    Of the gallant Third Ohio, Lieutenant-Colonel Bell,
      So like in shaggy ruggedness a mountain full of lairs
That when they cheered, you never knew the Buckeyes from
      the bears?
Ah! they loved the River Danger as Satan loves to sin,
Just drew their belts another hole, and then they waded in —
Waist-deep, chin-deep, the fellows went, nor drew a doubting
      breath,
No halting for an order nor touch of hat to Death!
"Go in!" and "Third Ohio!" their battle-cry and faith.

II.

Their talk was rough as bowlders are, and when they named
      the Flag
They christened it "Old Glory" or just "That blessed rag:"
Somebody fell —"passed in his checks" was all they had to say;

"God's country" was the happy land of "boiled shirts" every
    day;
They told of "wooden overcoats," and rude board coffins meant,
And thought they were a snugger fit than any Sibley tent;
But count the ragged blouses up, be sure the tale is true,
Each hides a handful of a heart beneath the tattered blue
That always played the Forward, March! and never beat tattoo.

III.

One Derby day they rode a raid and never drew the rein;
They rode as if they never meant to ride that route again.
Like long, clean sweep of trenchant blade where bonny flags
    burned blue,
And not a rift in all the field to let a star-beam through.
Down came a mantle broad and deep as comes the dusk of night,
In folds of gray and butternut, and swept them out of sight,
And swept them from their saddle-bows, and set their faces South,
And made a Daniel of the troop for Richmond's lion mouth,
And shriveled shut the bannered stars like daisies in a drouth.

IV.

"But why not tell it as it was?" I hear a fellow shout,
"Just make a finish of the thing, and say they bowled us out —
"One swallow, and the regiment was fairly gobbled up —

"Scooped by the blasted Johnny Rebs like water in a cup.

"They brushed us clean of cavalry, the infantry of clothes,

"And left the Third Ohio boys as naked as a nose."

For heavy baggage only hearts, each haversack was lank,

Nor flag nor fife to cheer along the dull, disastered rank;

Ah! deader than the March in Saul a canteen's empty clank.

V.

Along the road the weary miles lay quivering in the sun,

While naked Noon, with brazen blows, did weld them into one,

That naked feet must measure off before the work was done.

The days and boys crept slowly on — 'twas thirst and starve
    and tramp,

Until they tumbled, supperless, beside a Southern camp.

The Fifty-fourth Virginians came, like long-flanked leopard cats,

With dingy pipes of corn-cob in their shapeless, battered hats,

And, lean as stakes, they stood around and watched the novel
    sight

Of colors struck and empty hands, and Yankees "flying light."

VI.

Not long they gazed, but bolted with an "Old Dominion" whoop,

Promoted in a twinkling to a commissary troop!

You heard the clink of coffee-mills, the merry bayonet stroke,

The camp was turbaned like a Turk with wreaths of cedar smoke;
Then came the clang of frying-pan, the kettle's tambourine,
They routed out the lazy fires and tucked the "dodgers" in;
The martyred bacon made complaint and clouds of incense
    rose —
Oh! sweeter than the censer's swing to gain a soul's repose,
The Boys in Gray forgot that night the Boys in Blue were foes!

VII.

So sped the night in brotherhood, and when the dawning came,
They tucked two figures in their hearts — two figures and a
    name —
And hand met hand in soldier grip, no word of courtly thanks,
One said, "Good-by, Virginia," and one, "Light out, you Yanks."
Still war's wild weather ruled the year. November to July,
Deep thunders in the Cumberlands and lightnings in the sky.
The raiders were their own again, to Lookout back they came,
They told the tale a thousand times, it ended all the same;
The "Fifty-fourth Virginia" toast set hearts and cheeks a-flame,
And cheers flew wild, like sparks of fire—two figures and a name!

VIII.

The Hawk's Nest hatched great broods of blue; they chipped
    the butternut shell,
And fluttered up the rugged Ridge against the gates of hell —

How fierce and grand the flight and swoop let Chattanooga tell.
Lo! 'mid the captives whirling down, their faces to the North,
All wrapped like kittens in a cloak, Virginia's Fifty-fourth!

"THE BOYS IN GRAY FORGOT THAT NIGHT THE BOYS IN BLUE WERE FOES."

With bodies lean and faces long, they trailed in straggling rank,
And clustered like bepollened bees upon the river bank.
There, on the lazy Tennessee, the Third Ohio lay,
From Kelly's poor old Ferry a rifle-shot away.

The sturdy boys were "keeping house," amid the mountain
    glooms,
And smoky cones of Sibley tents, like rainy nights' mushrooms,
Had spread their gray umbrellas, with narrow streets between,
And the flicker of a bayonet, the glitter of canteen
As flitting spots of indigo pinked out the living green.

IX.

A lounging Buckeye took a look, saw "Old Virginia" come,
And broke for camp with lively feet, as drumsticks beat a drum.
Before he struck the picket-line he emptied every tent,
He never stayed for stock or stone, but shouted as he went —
What golden bugles should have blown and made a "joyful
    noise":
"THE FIFTY-FOURTH VIRGINIA IS AT THE FERRY, BOYS!"
Three minutes and the camp had swarmed: they bought the
    sutler out,
And brought their treasures to the light, and strewed them
    round about,
And nothing but a night surprise could raise so wild a rout.

X.

The kettles filled with Araby upon their muskets swung;
A bag of "hard-tack," tough as tiles, upon a shoulder slung;
A slab of bacon, broad and brown, as if it came from mill,

And so the laden caravan went filing down the hill.

The hosts were guests, the guests were hosts, and this alone
    was new,

The standard blazed with all its stars *above* the "bonny blue."

"AND SO THE LADEN CARAVAN WENT FILING DOWN THE HILL."

With winking camp-fires' dancing lights and dewdrops' beaded
    shine,

The night-air mantled rich and red as old Madeira wine,

Toned down the mellow picture, and made it half divine.

Oh! sweeter than the censer's swing to gain a soul's repose,

The Boys in Blue forgot that night the Boys in Gray were foes!

XI.

Arms won the game at Mission Ridge and played the hand
  alone;

At Kelly's Ferry hearts were trumps and *everybody* won.

The drifting years, like thistledown, have glittered out of sight;

The boys are mustered out of life, let no man say "good-night!"

The Boys in Blue and Boys in Gray sleep peacefully together,

And God's own stars shine through the flag and make it
  pleasant weather.

I lay this old love-story down upon the breast of May,

And dare to hope its words are meet for Decoration Day.

I lay this ballad's homely flower upon some soldier's bed,

While Love's sweet rain is falling fast upon the speechless dead.

The rose's stain is not of blood.   Are lilies pale with fear?

Then sure this offering of mine will harm nobody here.

At Kelly's Ferry once again let all the people meet,

With blessings clustered round their hearts and blossoms at
  their feet,

Give thanks the graves have ebbed at last that broke in bil-
  lowed sod,

And make one grand Red-letter Day for manhood and for God.

THE BARK "TRUE LOVE."

THE bark "True Love" arrived in the Delaware in November last, direct from Greenland, with a cargo of cryolite — both cargo and craft queer as an old ballad. She had been in commission one hundred and six years, and, like "the old ship Zion," her timbers were all sound. With her tulip-shaped hull and her cumbrous bulwarks she seemed to have sailed out of another age into our own.

THE BARK "TRUE LOVE."

Christmas Eve, 1875.

I.

WITH tack and turn in the idle air
    What craft comes beating up the Bay,
Comes curtsying up the Delaware?
Ahoy, Three-master! whence away?
Like millers' wings, her canvas gray
Is opened wide in ghastly palms
To feel for wind among the calms.

II.

Her sides are curved like the splendid flower
    That sets on fire the tulip tree,
Between her teeth the trusty bower
    They planted last in nameless sea,—
    Ah, Hope takes root where'er it be!—
Plucked up a thousand times with song,
Swung like a charm, and borne along!

III.

I hear the flap of the languid sail,
    The drowsy creak of swaying yard —
I see the bunting's lazy trail,
    A figure mount the battered guard —
    The breeze is purring like a pard.
" How are ye named, O gray and quaint!
" From monarch dead, or faded saint?"

IV.

Then came the word from the master's mate,
    Then bounded back a trumpet gust
Of salt-sea air articulate
    In tones that grated rough with rust:
    " From no dead king or saintly dust —
" The bark 'True Love' from Labrador,
" Whose sun is cold as Kohinor!"

V.

Where stars show through like the points of spears
    And cling and shine in wounded night,
Impale a thousand frozen years
    And halt the ages dead and white —
    Where Arctic's ghostly anthracite,

" UNTRAVELED ANGELS HAVE BEEN SEEN
ACROSS THAT STRAIT AND IN THE SKIES
BY CHILDREN'S CLEAR AND NAKED EYES!"

The icebergs crash before the breeze,
Unmelted, alabaster seas!

VI.

"The bark 'True Love' left the Cape Farewell
    "With cryolite from Greenland's coast "—
"What's cryolite?" He strove to tell,
    But on she swept — the words were lost;
    The waves' white plumage glanced and tossed,
So bore away this Arctic dove
From Cape Farewell to "Brotherly Love."

VII.

Think of her sailing down the age
    Across the line, and sailing yet!
The ink has faded from the page
    Whereon her score of captains set
    Two thousand names old salts forget—
Not one of all who worked the ship
Now lingers on a human lip.

VIII.

And here SHE is with her timbers sound,
    Stout-hearted oak, all through and through,
As when the columns graced the ground

Where acorns fell and giants grew!
O boatswain shrill! pipe up the crew,
And bid some breezy ballad blow
They sang an hundred years ago!

IX.

Some Chevy Chase with its endless line
   That runs along the slender tune,
As runs the bright Madeira vine
   And wreathes the thirty days of June,—
   Or love-lorn maidens and the moon,—
Or Spanish Main, or Blackbeard rhyme
Of ocean's Paradise of crime.

X.

Aye, tumble up from the watch below,
   Ye square-built sea-dogs tough and true,
That sailed the young "Love" long ago!
   In trowsers broad and jackets blue,
   Tarpaulins brave with streamers new,
With waistband hitch, and backward scrape,
And fore-lock touch, they round the Cape
And take the Horn! Can spectres speak?
They shift the cargo in the cheek!

XI.

The sailor's knot at each rugged throat
 As bare and brown as signal gun,
The rolling gait they learned afloat,—
 Ah, old True Lovers every one!
 Good night! Turn in! The watch is done!
Sleep till the sea its dead gives up,
As bubbles rise in beaded cup.

XII.

Behold her now! the gallant craft,—
 Between her teeth the bone-white foam,
She shows old ocean's rabble raft
 Of tumbling billows' roll and comb,
 Her heels at last and scurries home!
From Northern Crown to Southern Cross,
From eider-duck to albatross!

XIII.

To some broad Bay with its breathless glass
 Think that you see her sailing in —
All things in pairs that thither pass,
 The clouds are twos — she and her twin!

In such a place to sigh were sin ;
'Twould mar the perfect marriage there,
'Twixt this in sea and that in air.

XIV.

When days in pairs with their mingled light
   Of silver dawn and golden set,
Strike through each thin, transparent night,
   As if God's pearls and rubies met
   And kindled on a coronet,
How *could* she sail from Paradise
For Cape Farewell and Arctic ice?
From Greenland to the Delaware
God speed the "True Love" everywhere !

XV.

Almost two thousand Christian years,
   And every year of all the host,
An older, grander craft appears
   And sails along the Planet's coast
   As silent as a passing ghost;
Silent, except one Song they sing
On board the flag-ship of the KING.

XVI.

Upon its bow is a swinging star,
   Its sails are like some evening clouds
With here and there a silver spar;
   Its deck is thronged with angel crowds,
   Like threads of mist its filmy shrouds,
Its masts are made of beams of moon,
Its lettered flags of golden noon.
STAR IN THE EAST! Behold the name
Emblazoned on the streamer's flame!

XVII.

It plies the glorious Strait between
   Cape Christmas Eve and Paradise;
Untraveled angels have been seen
   Across that Strait and in the skies
   By children's clear and naked eyes!
It is their only yearly line
Between the earth and shores divine.

XVIII.

That Song of theirs — will it ever wane,
   Or flow like Life's eternal river?
"GOOD WILL TO MEN," its sweet refrain,

Is set to the key "Forever."

Ah, narrow Strait two worlds to sever!

The Port of Peace and Perfect Day

Are just across the azure way;—

Whoever strikes his earthly tent,

We will not wonder that he went,

We will not say that he has died,

But only gone the other side.

THE PSALM-BOOK IN THE GARRET.

THE old garret with one almond eye in each gable was the memory of the homestead. The fashions of three generations, the bits of ancient furniture that somehow grew akin to them that used it, the rusty red cradle, the rush-bottomed chair, the long-handled warming-pan, the little foot-stove with a bail to it, the flaring leghorn, the bell-crowned beaver, the leather-bound book, the wheel, the reel, the distaff and the swifts — these, and a thousand things besides, may be forgotten below stairs, but they are sure to be remembered above. You can find them swung to the peak of the rafters, or chucked under the eaves, or strown along the oaken plate. They are all there. When I hear of the burning of an old mansion, I do not ask if they saved the silver, but did salvation reach the garret!

The long-winged psalm-book, "sung in" by people whose graves are hard to find, lies upon a beam, and beside it a withered, dusty bundle of summer savory that nobody remembers. A little way off is a wooden pitch-pipe about the color of a chestnut, that used to go a couple of seconds ahead of Braintree and the rest, and blow like a disconsolate wind at a key-hole.

But the world will keep the old tunes without the help of garrets. Nobody ever thinks in "the dead waste and middle of" December that there can ever be another blue-bird. But there can, and there will. When "the winter is over and gone" he is sure to drop out of the blue like a winged atom of live sky. So with the old tunes. They have a way of dying out of hearing now and then, but, for all that, they will meet us here and there on the way. St. Martin's, St. Thomas and St. Mary's are about as immortal as St. Matthew, St. Paul and St. John. Let us amend the beatitude of Christopher North and say, "Blessed be the memory of old songs and old singers forever!"

THE PSALM-BOOK IN THE GARRET.

A GARRET grows a human thing
    With lonely oriental eyes,
To whom confiding fingers bring
    The world in yesterday's disguise.

THE ORIENTAL EYE.

Ah, richer far than noontide blaze
    The soft gray silence of the air,
As if long years of ended days
    Had garnered all their twilights there.

The heart can see so clear and far
 In such a place, with such a light —
God counts His heavens star by star,
 And rains them down unclouded night.

Where rafters set their cobwebb'd feet
 Upon the rugged oaken ledge,
I found a flock of singers sweet,
 Like snow-bound sparrows in a hedge.

In silk of spider's spinning hid,
 A long and narrow Psalm-book lay;
I wrote a name upon the lid,
 Then brushed the idle dust away.

Ah, dotted tribe with ebon heads
 That climb the slender fence along!
As black as ink, as thick as weeds,
 Ye little Africans of song!

Who wrote upon this page "Forget
 Me Not?" These cruel leaves of old
Have crushed to death a violet —
 See here its spectre's pallid gold.

A penciled whisper during prayer

    Is that poor, dim and girlish word,

But ah, I linger longest where

    It opens of its own accord.

" YE LITTLE AFRICANS OF SONG."

These spotted leaves! How once they basked

    Beneath the glance of girlhood's eyes,

And parted to the gaze unasked,

    As spread the wings of butterflies.

The book falls open where it will —

    Broad on the page runs Silver Street!

That shining way to Zion's Hill

    Where base and treble used to meet.

I shake the leaves. They part at Mear —
   Again they strike the good old tune,
The village church is builded here,
   The twilight turns to afternoon.

Old house of Puritanic wood,
   Through whose unpainted windows streamed
On seats as primitive and rude
   As Jacob's pillow when he dreamed,

The white and undiluted day!
   Thy naked aisle no roses grace
That blossomed at the shuttle's play;
   Nor saints distempered bless the place.

Like feudal castles, front to front,
   In timbered oak of Saxon Thor,
To brave the siege and bear the brunt
   Of Bunyan's endless Holy War,

The pulpit and the gallery stand —
   Between the twain a peaceful space,
The prayer and praise on either hand,
   And girls and Gospel face to face.

I hear the reverend Elder say,

   "*Hymn fifty-first, long meter, sing!*"

I hear the Psalm-books' fluttered play

   Like flocks of sparrows taking wing.

THE PULPIT AND THE GALLERY.

Armed with a fork to pitch the tune,
  I hear the Deacon call "*Dundee!*"
And mount as brisk as Bonny Doon
  His "Fa, sol, la," and scent the key.

He "trees" the note for sister Gray;
  The old Scotch warbling strains begin;
The base of Bashan leads the way,
  And all the girls fall sweetly in.

How swells the hymn of heavenly love,
  As rise the tides in Fundy's Bay!
Till all the air below, above,
  Is sweet with song and — caraway!

A fugue let loose cheers up the place,
  With base and tenor, alto, air;
The parts strike in with measured grace,
  And something sweet is everywhere!

As if some warbling brood should build
  Of bits of tunes a singing nest,
Each bring the notes with which it thrilled
  And weave them in with all the rest!

The congregation rise and stand;
   Old Hundred's rolling thunder comes
In heavy surges, slow and grand,
   As beats the surf its solemn drums.

Now come the times when China's wail
   Is blended with the faint perfume
Of whispering crape and cloudy veil,
   That fold within their rustling gloom

Some wounded human mourning-dove,
   And fall around some stricken one
With nothing left alive to love
   Below the unregarded sun!

And now they sing a star in sight,
   The blessed Star of Bethlehem;
And now the air is royal bright
   With Coronation's diadem.

They show me spots of dimpled sod,
   They say the girls of old are there—
Oh, no, they swell the choirs of God,
   The dear old Songs are everywhere!

HOW THE BROOK WENT TO MILL.

I.

A RIFTED rock in a wooded hill,
    A spring within like a looking-glass,
    A nameless rill like a skein of rain
That showed as faint as a feeble vein,
And crept away in the tangled grass
With a voiceless flow and a wandering will,—
    The *wish-ton-wish* of a silken dress,
    The murmured tone of a maiden's "yes!"
    A thirsty ox could have quaffed it up,
    A boy dipped dry with a drinking cup!
      Broke in a brook the rill complete —
      Broke in a song the brook so fleet —
      Broke in a laugh the song so sweet!

II.

'Twas pebble, rubble, and fallen tree,
'Twas babble, double, through every mile;
It battled on with a shout and shock,

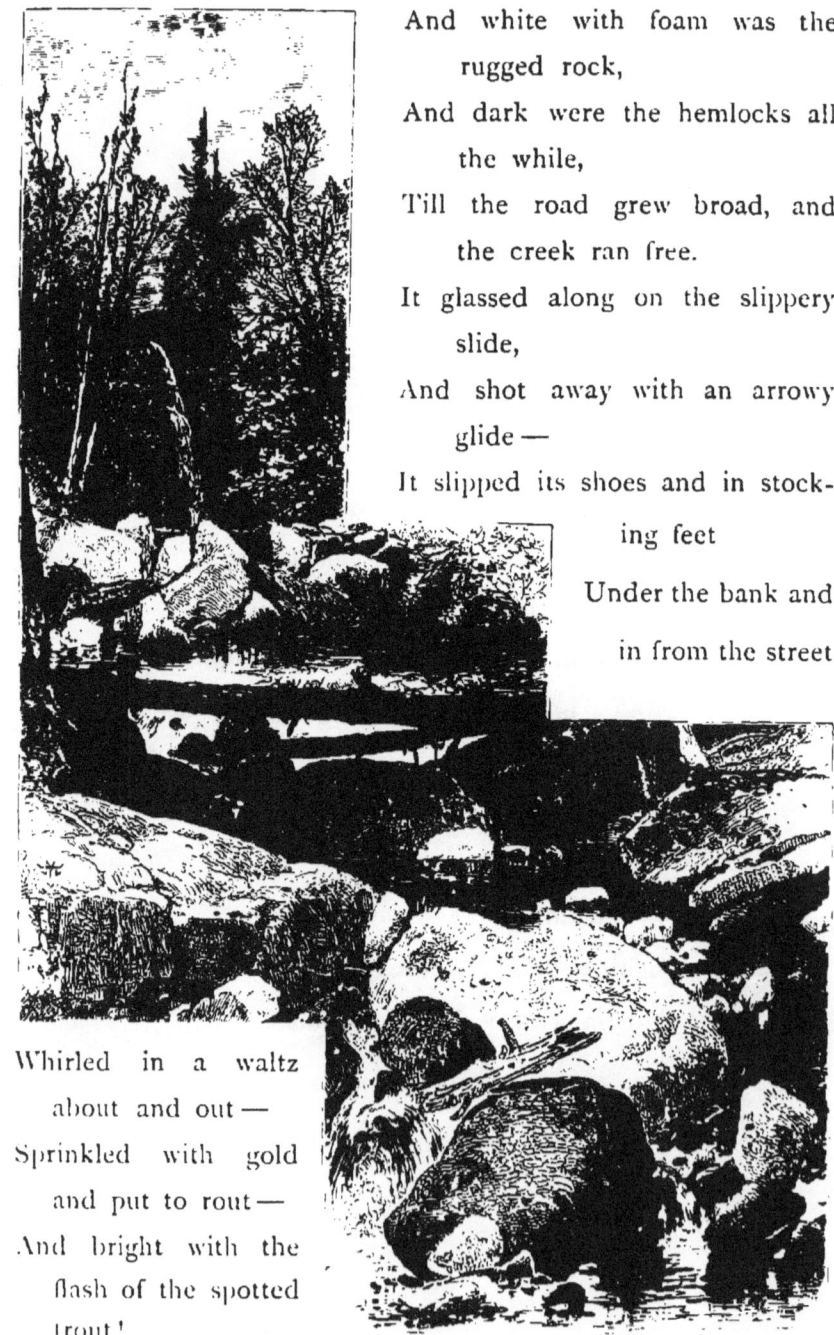

And white with foam was the rugged rock,
And dark were the hemlocks all the while,
Till the road grew broad, and the creek ran free.
It glassed along on the slippery slide,
And shot away with an arrowy glide —
It slipped its shoes and in stocking feet
Under the bank and in from the street

Whirled in a waltz about and out —
Sprinkled with gold and put to rout —
And bright with the flash of the spotted trout!

III.

It floats a name and it bears a boat;
'Tis Leonard's Creek and is bound for mill,
And makes you think, with its ripple and flow,—
So light it trips to the stones below
The rhythmic touch of the gay quadrille —
How her *fingers* went when they moved by note
   Through measures fine, as she marched them o'er
   The yielding plank of the ivory floor.
   Beneath the bridge with a rasping rush,
   A bird takes toll,—'tis a thirsty thrush,—
   It nears the Gulf of the hemlock night
   Where stars shine down in the mid-day light,
   It verges the brink of the shadow's lair,
   Stumbles and falls on the limestone stair!
      Clings to the mute and motionless edge —
      Tumbles and booms from ledge to ledge —
      Thunders and blunders down to the sedge!

THE MILLER AND THE MILL.

A RIVER and a brook ran across my boyhood's world;
lively fellows they were, and things to thank God for.
The one rambled through pastures and meadows, among the
buttercups and strawberries, and turned shingle wheels and
floated boats that suggested the slipper of Cinderella, and wet
boys' feet and their trowsers withal, even to the waistbands,
glassed out in the spring rains like the Zuider Zee, and sub-
mitted to be dammed without a murmur.

The other rattled down the roughest, crookedest piece of
road you ever saw, and quarreled with banks and wrangled
with rocks and foamed over fallen logs as green as lizards,
and plunged into hemlock shadows it never could get rid of,
slipped over the broad flat pavements and tumbled down stairs
at last at the foot of the mill. The old mill with its rumble
and grumble, its ghostly corners, its powdery floors, and its dim
gray look, as if lost in a fog that never lifts, is there yet, rumbling and grumbling still. It hums like a king-bee in the nest
of a village. The great wheel in its damp dungeon below day-
time, gives way as of old beneath the tread of water, like a
flight of stairs forever tumbling down.

The mill was our only enchanted castle, and nobody has ruined it by improvement. As of old,

> " Water runneth by the mill
> The miller wots not of."

What treasures of childhood came home in the grists; the turnover bundled in a coverlid, tucked in with a thumb and plump with happiness; the golden samp; the corner lot of Johnny-cake; the acrobatic flap-jack, and the twisted dough-nut. But the charm of them has vanished. Happiness is rarer and costlier. The old miller has laid off his dusty clothes for garments of white, and strange hands take toll.

THE MILLER AND THE MILL.

I.

THE roar came up in a misty cloak
    Whose skirt was trimmed with the swan's-down
        foam,
Beside the mill with its window'd wall
Of rusty red as it loomed so tall.
The wheel was still in its dank, dim room,
The air as whist as a wreath of smoke,
The tangled light through the cobwebs fell,
The mill was as dumb as a heather-bell!
The dusty miller was leaning o'er
The lower half of the battened door,
Thinking the things he *always* thought,
Tolling the grist no man had brought,
Counting the dreams that came to nought.

II.

He saw four butterflies winged in white
That fluttered over the wayside pool,
They looked like bits of an old love-note
To Lucy Jones, and the first he wrote
But never sent to the Flower of school —
"What if he had?" and "Perhaps she might!"
He saw four butterflies winged in gold
And thought what things the "perhaps" might fold —
A woman's foot on the powdered sill
With arch enough for a running rill,
To walk his world and — he thought again
How blossoms show in the route of rain —
Make summer-time till the first snow-fall.
Perhaps and Might! How they puzzle all!

Jogging along a horse came slow,
Boy was aloft and bag below,
Calliper legs and head of tow.

III.

The miller starts from the faded dream,
A lever creaks and he lifts the gate.
The rumbling flood in the frothy flume

Is rolling through to the twilight room

In whirls and swirls at a reckless rate

The rustic strength of the headlong stream.

"HE SAW FOUR BUTTERFLIES WINGED IN GOLD."

A storm of rain in the chamber dim!
A mighty swing of a giant limb!
The Wheel is washing his naked arms!
The mill is alive with the strange alarms!
A lazy log has just turned over.

The mill is full of a thousand things,
They tramp with feet and they hum with wings —
A troop has halted awhile to feed,
Old Pan has come with his drowsy reed.
Hark! Bees abroad from a field of clover!
A flock of grouse with a frightened whir!
A Scotch brigade with a Tweedside burr!

Two wheels lay hold with their iron teeth
And turn a shaft that is hung beneath,
With a jumbling thump of the tumbling bolt,
Like the awkward trot of a bare-foot colt;
In swaying glide are the leathern bands,
The hoppers jar with their palsied hands,
Forever spilling the grists of grain
In rattling showers like frozen rain,
While face to face with its gritty mate
The mill-stone whirls with a grinding grate.

What might be laid in a castle's wall
Is twirled as light as a parasol!

And out from the Rock, as once of old,
A streamlet flows in its white or gold!

Busy as bees when the buckwheat blows
Are the little buckets that run in rows
Up stairs and down with a sparrow's weight,
A tiny drift of the dainty freight.
The place is thrilled with a rumbling tread,
The air is gray with the ghost of bread!
Dizzy and busy, above, below,
Lydian river and floury flow —
Corn in the gold and wheat in the snow.

IV.

The old gray mill is yet murmuring on,
The brook brawls down through the limestone street,
The girls that blossomed around the door
And hid and sought till the grist-snowed floor
Was printed off with their merry feet
Like notes of music — the girls are gone!
The miller said that he always heard

The slender song of the outside bird
Through the grumbling roll of the whirling mill,
He never heard when the wheels were still.
Perhaps — why not? — through the anthem grand
He helps to chant in the Better Land,
The mill's old murmuring monotone
May now steal up to his ear alone,
Bringing a breath of the Savior's Prayer —
Droning the base to the angels' air —
Hum of the Mill in the golden choir!

THE OLD STATE ROAD.

THE old State Road from Utica, New York, to Lake Ontario was, like Jordan, "a hard road to travel." Macadamized with rocks that never felt a hammer; bordered with bowlders and mayweed in summer, and in winter with drifts of snow that left the country as fenceless as the Arctic Ocean; rising and falling with the high hills and the deep valleys like a tremendous sea; the most like a liquid when it had a solid's three dimensions,—length, breadth and thickness,—with all this, it had a charm for "us boys" that the Appian Way or the sheep paths up the Hill of Science never possessed, for it led out into the unseen world, and people went by stage — the yellow, egg-shaped, rollicking coach that smelled of tar, leather, buffalo robes and reeking horses, but then no triumphal chariot of classic story was ever half so grand.

Of that road John Benjamin, Driver, was hero and king. The breadth of his realm was as far as he could see on both sides of the way, and his subjects were all the people. His name, as here given, is exactly half true, and that is about all we can say of most history. A genial, hearty, tough fellow was John Benjamin. A reinsman without a master, he could get more volleys of small-arms out of the, farther end of a whip-lash and a skein of silk than any man going; he could turn a straight tin horn into a key-bugle; he believed in oats, and next to a matched and mettled four-in-hand, he admitted that man was the noblest animal on earth.   He knew everybody, and was not above a nod to little boys, and a smile for slips of girls, even if he could count their toes any summer day as they stood by the road side.   A man might be forgiven for being unacquainted with Apollo, Jehu or Palinurus, but not with John Benjamin.   Not a lad in the country but meant to be a man and a driver himself.   Not a lass but wished she could ride in John Benjamin's coach on her wedding day.

The coaches are all wrecked.   The Drivers are all gone; but the stage road remains.   I got glimpses of it a while ago, as I went scurrying along by rail, and of dilapidated stage-houses, as gray as wasps' nests, and as empty as martin-boxes in mid winter.   "So runs the world away!"

THE OLD STATE ROAD.

CUT through the green wilderness down to the ground,
　　Straight over the hills by the route of the crow,
　Now black as the bird, where the hemlocks abound,
　Then through the dim pines, half as white as the snow,
By a cataract's track sunk away to the gulf
That yawned grim and dark as the mouth of a wolf,
Up hill and down dale like the trail of a brave,
From Mohawk's wet marge to Ontario's wave,
When the world was in forest, the hamlet in grove,
Ran the stormy State Road where old Benjamin drove.

The rude rugged bridges all growled at the stage,
　The rough rolling ridges all gave it a lift,
You read off the route like a line on a page,
　Then dropped out of day into twilight and rift!
Through the sloughs of October it heavily rolled
　And lurched like a ship that is mounting a sea,
O'er rattling macadams of torrents untold,
　Now in silence and sand midway to the knee.

It visioned the night with its yellow-eyed lamps
Like creatures that prowl out of gun-shot of camps,
When plunging along in the gloom of the swamps,
With halt, jolt and thump and the driver's "ahoy!"
It struck with a bounce on the ribbed corduroy,
And from hemlock to hemlock, log in and log out,
The coach jumped and jounced in a trip-hammer bout —
Through Gothic old chasms that swallowed the night,
Out into the clearings all golden with light.
Where flocks of white villages lay in the grass
And watched for the stage and its cargo to pass.

JOHN BENJAMIN, DRIVER.

THE boys and the girls all abroad in high feather,
The heads of the horses all tossing together,
Flinging flakes of white foam like snow in wild weather,
All swinging their silk like tassels of corn,
'Twas Benjamin's time! And he whipped out the horn!
'Twas the drone of king bees and a myriad strong —
'Twas *fanfare!* and *fanfare!* with a bugle's prolong,
Chanticleer! Chan-ti-cleer! I am coming along!

The bellows dropped down with a vanishing snore,
The smith in black crayon gave the anvil the floor

"RIGHT-ABOUT WITH A DASH CAME THE FOUR-IN-HAND."

And leaned on his sledge in the cave of a door;
The landlord in slippers cut away at the heel
Shuffled out on the stoop at the rattle of wheel,
Click-click — went the gates, and like yarn from a reel,
Smiling women wound out and looked down the street
Where the driver swung plumb in his oriole seat,
The mail, chained and padlocked, tramped under his feet.

He tightens the reins and whirls off with a fling
From the roof of the coach his ten feet of string;
The invisible fire-works rattle and ring,
Torpedoes exploding in front and in rear,
A Fourth of July every day in the year!
Now lightly he flicks the " nigh " leader's left ear,
Gives the wheelers a neighborly slap with the stock,
They lay back their ears as the coach gives a rock
And strike a square trot in the tick of a clock!

There's a jumble, a jar and a gravelly trill
In the craunch of the wheels on the slate-stone hill
That grind up the miles like a grist in a mill.

He touches the bay and he talks to the brown,
Sends a token of silk, a word and a frown
To the filly whose heels are too light to stay down.

Clouds of dust roll behind with two urchins inside
That tow by the straps, as the jolly-boats ride,
From the boot rusty-brown like an elephant's hide.
With a sharp jingling halt he brings up at the door,
A surge to the coach like a ship by the shore,
He casts off the lines and his journey is o'er.

If king were to banter, would Benjamin trade
His box for a knighthood, his whip for the blade
That should make him Sir John by some grand accolade?

Ah, few whips alive in their cleverest mood
Can write with a coach as old Benjamin could,
And you ought to have seen the sixteen feet
With their iron shoes on the stricken stone
When they waltzed around in the narrow street
To a time and a tune that were all their own,
Like the short sharp clicks of the castanet
By the Moorish girls in a dancing set,
When, as free as the sweep of a wizard's wand,
Right-about with a dash came the four-in-hand!
'Twas crackle of buckskin and sparkle of fire,
And never a rasp of a grazing tire,
As he cut a clean 6 and swept a bold 8,
Like a boy that is trying his brand-new slate!

JOHN BENJAMIN'S PICTURE.

I see him to-day all equipped for the snow
In a wonderful coat that falls to his heels,
With its ripple of capes on his shoulders a-flow,
And a plump visored cap that once was a seal's
Drawn snug to his eye-brows down over his head;
In gloves of tough buckskin so wrinkled and brown,
With muffler begirt, an equator of red!
A shawl round his neck like a turban slipped down;
A couple of cubs are his buffalo shoes
Asleep on the mail-bag that carries the news.
All through of a size, in his Esquimaux guise,
He read off the road and he breasted the storm,
No sign of the man but his hands and his eyes,
His heart below frost — ah! it always kept warm.
"Afraid?"   If bright Phœbus had told him to try
His horses of fire down the steep of the sky,
With the motto *Ich dien,* — I faithfully serve, —
He would grasp the gold reins, no falter of nerve,
And, foot on the brake, he would drive down the Blue
Without breaking an axle or losing a shoe!
A touch of North-easters had frosted his tones, —
He always must talk so his leaders could hear, —

"I SEE HIM TO-DAY ALL EQUIPPED FOR THE SNOW."

Ah, men preach from grand pulpits and sit upon thrones,
Whose vision of duty was never so clear!
He loved the old route with its hemlock and rock,
Its sprinkle of mayweed, the breath of its hills,
The girls trailing out in bare feet from the flock
That ran alongside when the horses would walk,
Till they wore a small path like the travel of rills!

Ah, Hero of boyhood! Asleep in thy grave,
Last Station of all on humanity's route,
In measureless peace where the Lombardies wave,
But time and its tempests have blotted it out.
I letter his name on the Way Bill of Death
To tell who he was that is waiting beneath:

Good night to John Benjamin, King of the Road!—
Who sleeps till the blast of the bugle of God.
In feverish noon, on the Highway of Strife,
Make the driver's old rule the law of your life:
Keep the track if you can, but mid-day or mid-night,
Whatever you do, always turn to the right!

THE OLD BARN.

GENUINE boys take to barns as ducks take to water; not dandies of barns, disguised with paint and crowned with observatories, but roomy, gray, *sincere* fellows, with the perpetual twilight, and the big beam, and the broad bay, billowy with sweet hay, and the granary with its delicious Radcliffian gloom, and the threshing-floor where flails fell, and feet danced after the husking, to the measure of Money Musk; barns with no adorning save a diamond in each gable to let the swallows through, and a shingle chanticleer upon the ridge that creaks but never crows; barns with musical roofs and twittering eaves, where the rainy days are the pleasantest in all the calendar.

Here, if anywhere, a boy slips off the harness of constraint and the shoes of propriety that he wears in the house, and turns himself out to grass, leastwise to hay, and climbs like the ambitious bean of Jack the Giant-Killer, and leaps like the frogs of Egypt, and makes a hoop of himself, and lets out his quicksilver life at every toe and finger end like sparks of lightning from the points of an electric wheel, and gives tongue like the hounds of Actæon, and, all the while like the righteous, "with none to molest or make him afraid!"

Later, he leads the dance with some belle of the husking on the oaken floor, by the twinkle of tin lanterns, and the eyes of the astonished horses shining in the stalls, and the fowls winking slow from the high perch.

The relentless years go on, and the man makes thought-pilgrimage to the homestead, but he reaches it by way of the barn, and he tarries there and enters it, sometimes, and beholds his own boyhood come to resurrection in the old twilight amid the shouts of dead comrades, the flutter of dead birds, and the fragrance of clover that perished full forty mowings ago. The same bee in black velvet and yellow trimmings drifts in his saucy way over the door-sill. The same red fanning-mill stands beside the granary door with a hen's nest in the hopper. The same bars of dusty sunshine strike through the creviced wall and slant across the bay. There is a strange mingling of the living and the dead. A man can slip back into childhood faster in a barn than in a human dwelling. There are no new fashions in furniture. The doves and the swallows are in the same old clothes, and the clips of the broad-ax show as plain as ever on the cobwebbed beams.

If barns are the Meccas of rural boyhood they were the first Christian churches of the young wilderness. Honored is the barn above all the palaces of earth, for in it the Savior of the world was born, and the manger was His cradle.

THE OLD BARN.

A GREAT dim barn with the fragrant bay
Up to the beam with the winter's hay,
And its shrunken siding wasp-nest gray;

Where the cracks between run up and down,
Like the narrow lines in a striped gown,
And let in light of a golden brown.

They are bars of bronze,— they are silver snow,—
As the sunshine falls, or sifting slow
The white flakes drift on the wealth below

Of the clover blossoms faint with June
That had heard all day his small bassoon
As the ground-bee played his hum-drum tune.

Ah, what would you give to have again
Your pulse keep time with the dancing rain,
When flashing through at the diamond pane

You saw the swallows' rapier wings
As they cut the air in ripples and rings
And laughed and talked like human things?

When they drank each other's health, you thought,—
For the creak of the corks you surely caught,—
And all day long at their cabins wrought,

Till the mud-walled homes with a foreign look,
A pictured street in an Aztec book,
Began to show in each rafter'd nook?

Never again! Alack and alas!
Like a breath of life on the looking-glass,
Like a censer smoke, the pictures pass.

THE FLAILS.

"WELL, Jack and Jim," said the farmer gray,
"The flour is out and we'll *thrash* to-day!"—
A hand is on the granary door,
And a step is on the threshing floor,—
It is not his and it is not theirs,—
He went above by the Golden Stairs;
The boys are men and the nicknames grown,
'Tis James Esquire and Reverend John.

"WHEN THE BOUNCING KERNELS, BRIGHT AND BROWN,
LEAP LIGHTLY UP AS THE FLAILS COME DOWN."

How they waltzed the portly sheaves about
As they loosed their belts, and shook them out
In double rows on the threshing floor
Clean as the deck of a Seventy-four!
When down the midst in a tawny braid
The sculptured heads of the straw were laid,
It looked a poor man's family bed!
Ah, more than that, 'twas a carpet fair
Whereon the flails with their measured tread
Should time the step of the answered prayer,
"Give us this day our daily bread!"
Then the light half-whirl and the hickory clash
With the full free swing of a buckskin lash,
And the trump — tramp — trump, when the bed is new,
In regular, dull, monotonous stroke,
And the click — clack — click, on the floor of oak
When the straw grows thin and the blows strike through;
And the French-clock tick to the dancing feet
With the small tattoo of the driven sleet,
When the bouncing kernels bright and brown
Leap lightly up as the flails come down.

THE FANNING MILL.

HANG up the flails by the big barn-door!
Bring out the mill of the one-boy power!
Nothing at all but a breeze in a box,
Clumsy and red it rattles and rocks,

"NOTHING AT ALL BUT A BREEZE IN A BOX."

Sieves to be shaken and hopper to feed,
A Chinaman's hat turned upside down,
The grain slips through at a hole in the crown —
Out with the chaff and in with the speed!

The crank clanks round with a boy's quick will,
The fan flies fast till it fills the mill
With its breezy vanes, as the whirled leaves fly
In an open book when the gust goes by;
And the jerky jar and the zig-zag jolt
Of the shaken sieves, and the jingling bolt,
And the grate of cogs and the axle's clank
And the rowlock jog of the crazy crank,
And the dusty rush of the gusty chaff
The worthless wreck of the harvest's raff,
And never a lull, the brisk breeze blows
From the troubled grain its tattered clothes,
Till tumbled and tossed it downward goes
The rickety route by the rackety stair,
Clean as the sand that the simoon snows,
And drifts at last in a bank so fair
You *know* you have found the Answered Prayer!

THE OLD BARN'S TENANTRY.

The rooster stalks on the manger's ledge,
He has a tail like a scimitar's edge,

A marshal's plume on his Afghan neck,
An admiral's stride on his quarter deck.

THE OLD BARN'S TENANTRY.

He rules the roost and he walks the bay,
With a dreadful cold and a Turkish way,

Two broadsides fires with his rapid wings —
This sultan proud, of a line of kings,—

One guttural laugh, four blasts of horn,
Five rusty syllables rouse the morn!

The Saxon lambs in their woolen tabs
Are playing school with their a, b, abs:

A, e! I, o! All the cattle spell
Till they make the blatant vowels tell,

And a half-laugh whinny fills the stalls
When down in the rack the clover falls.

A dove is waltzing around his mate,
Two chevrons black on his wings of slate,

And showing off with a wooing note
The satin shine of his golden throat.

It is Ovid's "Art of Love" re-told
In a binding fine of blue and gold!

Ah, the buxom girls that helped the boys —
The nobler Helens of humbler Troys —

"I HEAR THE LATCH WHEN THE EAR IS RED."

As they stripped the husks with rustling fold
From eight-rowed corn as yellow as gold,

By the candle-light in pumpkin bowls,
And the gleams that showed fantastic holes

In the quaint old lantern's tattooed tin,
From the hermit glim set up within;

By the rarer light in girlish eyes
As dark as wells, or as blue as skies.

I hear the laugh when the ear is red,
I see the blush with the forfeit paid,

The cedar cakes with the ancient twist,
The cider cup that the girls have kissed,

And I see the fiddler through the dusk
As he twangs the ghost of " Money Musk ! "

The boys and girls in a double row
Wait face to face till the magic bow

Shall whip the tune from the violin,
And the merry pulse of the feet begin.

MONEY MUSK.

In shirt of check and tallowed hair
The fiddler sits in the bulrush chair
Like Moses' basket stranded there
  On the brink of Father Nile.
He feels the fiddle's slender neck,
Picks out the notes with thrum and check,
And times the tune with nod and beck,
  And thinks it a weary while.

All ready! Now he gives the call,
Cries, "*Honor to the ladies!*" All
The jolly tides of laughter fall
  And ebb in a happy smile.

D-o-w-n comes the bow on every string,
"*First couple join right hands and swing!*"
And light as any blue-bird's wing
  "*Swing once and a half times round!*"
Whirls Mary Martin all in blue —
Calico gown and stockings new,
And tinted eyes that tell you true,
  Dance all to the dancing sound.

She flits about big Moses Brown
Who holds her hands to keep her down
And thinks her hair a golden crown

    And his heart turns over once!
His cheek with Mary's breath is wet,
It gives a second somerset!
He means to win the maiden yet,

    Alas, for the awkward dunce!

"Your stoga boot has crushed my toe!"
"I'd rather dance with one-legged Joe,"
"You clumsy fellow!" "*Pass below!*"

    And the first pair dance apart.
Then "*Forward six!*" advance, retreat,
Like midges gay in sunbeam street
'Tis Money Musk by merry feet

    And the Money Musk by heart!

"*Three quarters round your partner swing!*"
"*Across the set!*" The rafters ring,
The girls and boys have taken wing

    And have brought their roses out!
'Tis "*Forward six!*" with rustic grace
Ah, rarer far than —"*Swing to place!*"

"'TIS MONEY MUSK BY MERRY FEET."

Than golden clouds of old point-lace
　　They bring the dance about.

Then clasping hands all —"*Right and left!*"
All swiftly weave the measure deft
Across the woof in living weft
　　And the Money Musk is done!
Oh, dancers of the rustling husk,
Good night, sweethearts, 'tis growing dusk,
Good night for aye to Money Musk,
　　For the heavy march begun!

SILVER WEDDING DAY.

A SILVER wedding means two starry days: one trembling with the ineffable grace of youth through the dews of the early East; the other, clear, calm, serene, shining down upon the middle of the world. "One star differeth from another star in glory."

A slender, smooth-faced friend, who could tumble types into position as a French clock ticks, helped the writer commit his first typographical sin by printing a book for him. It was born of an old hand-press, and bound to a board like a small papoose, in the year eighteen hundred and — well, no matter, it was before the first starry day had dawned. The friend turned editor, general, Congressional Representative, and at last turned his twenty-fifth wedding day. And so from the hills of Chenango to the Lakes of Wisconsin, a greeting went to him of the silver beard and the silver day. But these silver-mounted annuals glitter all along the year. The clock of the age strikes quarters for some pair every day. And so, from this pebble of a poem flung into the river Time, a concentric ring may ripple out perhaps and touch yet other hearts with its little wave of cheer.

SILVER WEDDING DAY.

———

I.

BREAK cloudless bright, thy Silver Day,
    Old friend of boyhood and of prime!
Bind August sheaves with flowers of May,
    And ring the silver bells of Time!

II.

The years, like planets, rise and set,
    We bid some royal day good-by —
Stand fast, dear heart, that day may yet
    Dawn grandly up the Eastern sky.

III.

Oh, Wedding Morn! as once before
    Upon the rose of 'forty-nine,
On silver bride of 'seventy-four
    In breathless splendor rise and shine!

IV.

Three bridemaids stand and bless the place :
　　A stately girl with step of air —
Another with uplifted face,
　　And parted lips and golden hair —

V.

And one appareled all in white
　　Save where the rose shows through the cheek,
Save where the eyes flash blue and bright
　　And look the vow she cannot speak.

VI.

I know them all ! Red, white, and blue
　　Are Love's own colors everywhere,
And there smiles Hope as young as dew,
　　With tangled sunshine in her hair.

VII.

And grander than the graceful twain,
　　Lo, queenly Faith, whose heavenly eyes
Discern the clear *beyond* the rain
　　And catch their tint from cloudless skies.

THE SILVER WEDDING.

VIII.

Joy to the Wife who stands beside
    That trefoil group of Paradise!
God bless the bridegroom and the bride!
    As Thou hast blest, so bless them twice,

IX.

With rounded days, serene as June,
    That flowers the year in tropic clime,
Through life's long summer afternoon,
    Like perfect words in perfect time.

X.

Chenango's greensward breaks to-day
    As grandly round the scalloped sky,
Her billows lift the rocks of gray,
    Their wooded crests as bravely fly,
As when they kept the *world* away,
    These breathless seas that never die!

XI.

This troubled earth is troubled still,
    The brooks yet run their pebbly route,
I count each old familiar hill,
    But how "God's acre" widens out!

XII.

The marble doors bear household words
    That charm our daily speech no more,
Strange that the sweet old songs of birds
    Outlive the name that beauty bore —

XIII.

That youth and genius should have died
    Like waves along some drowsy shore,
And yet these graceful elms abide
    And lilacs bloom beside the door.

XIV.

The sunshine has a lonely look,
    The dew has vanished from the sod,
The past a worn and tattered book
    With little left but love and God.

XV.

Whoever dies, these live right on!
    Why play the gloomy March in Saul?
Be green, ye graves! Be bright, oh, sun!
    Life is not lived without ye all.

XVI.

Be girded up, oh, heart of mine,
  And wing this greeting to the West;
Old comrade of the days lang syne,
  Be thou and thine forever blest!

THE SPINNING WHEEL.

A WHITE pine floor and a low-ceiled room,
 A wheel and a reel and a great brown loom,
 The windows out and the world in bloom,—

A pair of "swifts" in the corner, where
The grandmother sat in her rush-wrought chair,
And pulled at the distaff's tangled hair,

And sang to herself as she spun the tow
While "the little wheel" ran as soft and low
As muffled brooks where the grasses grow,
And lie one way with the water's flow.

As the Christ's field lilies free from sin,
So she grew like them when she ceased to spin,
Counted her "knots" and handed them in!

"The great wheel" rigged in its harness stands—
A three-legg'd thing with its spindle and bands;—

And the slender spokes, like the willow wands
That spring so thick in the low, wet lands,
Turn dense at the touch of a woman's hands.

As the wheel whirls swift, how rank they grow!
But how sparse and thin when the wheel runs slow
Forward and backward, and to and fro!

There's a heap of rolls like clouds in curl,
And a bright-faced, springy, barefoot girl —
She gives a touch and a careless whirl,

She holds a roll in her shapely hand
That the sun has kissed and the wind has fanned,
And its mate obeys the wheel's command.

There must be wings on her rosy heel!
And there must be bees in the spindled steel!
A thousand spokes in the dizzy wheel!

Have you forgotten the left-breast knock
When you bagged the bee in the hollyhock,
And the angry burr of an ancient clock,

All ready to strike, came out of the mill,
Where covered with meal the rogue was still,
Till it made your thumb and finger thrill?

It is one, two, three — the roll is caught;

'Tis a backward step and the thread is taut,

A hurry of wheel and the roll is wrought!

"SHE GIVES A TOUCH AND A CARELESS WHIRL."

'Tis one, two, three, and the yarn runs on,

And the spindle shapes like a white-pine cone,

As even and still as something grown.

The barefoot maiden follows the thread
Like somebody caught and tether'd and led
Up to the buzz of the busy head.

With backward sweep and willowy bend
Monarch would borrow if maiden could lend,
She draws out the thread to the white wool's end,

From English sheep of the old-time farm,
With their legs as fair as a woman's arm,
And faces white as a girl's alarm.

She breaks her thread with an angry twang,
Just as if at her touch a harp-string rang
And keyed to the quaint old song she sang

That came to a halt on her cherry lip
While she tied one knot that never could slip,
And thought of *another*, when her ship,—

All laden with dreams in splendid guise,—
Should sail right out of the azure skies
And a lover bring with great brown eyes!

Ah, broad the day but her work was done —
Two "runs" by reel! She had twisted and spun
Her two score "knots" by set of sun.

With her one, two, three, the wheel beside,
And the three, two, one, of her backward glide,
So to and fro in calico pride
Till the bees went home and daytime died!

Her apron white as the white sea foam,
She gathered the wealth of her velvet gloom,
And railed it in with a tall back-comb.

She crushed the dews with her naked feet,
The track of the sun was a golden street,
The grass was cool and the air was sweet.

The girl gazed up at the mackerel sky,
And it looked like a *pattern* lifted high,
But she never dreamed of angels nigh,

And she spoke right out: "Do just see there!
"What a blue and white for the clouded pair
"I'm going to knit for my Sunday wear!"

The wheel is dead and the bees are gone,
And the girl is dressed in a silver lawn,
And her feet are shod with golden dawn.

From a wind-swung tree that waves before,

A shadow is dodging in at the door,—

Flickering ghost on the white-pine floor,—

And the cat, unlearned in Shadow's law,

Just touched its edge with a velvet paw

To hold it still with an ivory claw!

But its spectral cloak is blown about,

And a moment more and the ghost is out,

And leaves us all in shadowy doubt

If ever it fell on floor at all,

Or if ever it swung along the wall,

Or whether a shroud or a phantom shawl!

Oh, brow that the old-time morning kissed!

Good night, my girl of the double and twist!

Oh, barefoot vision!   Vanishing mist!

MOWING.

I.

OH, days that are always dying,
　　Each turning its face to mine
Across the breadth of a life-time,
　　Like suns with their level shine
That set on a world divine!

II.

Sweet day of doom in the meadow
　　Most redolent day abroad,
When grasses, daisies and clover
　　All die like the Saints of God,
And fragrance floats in the sunshine
　　And eloquence fills the sod.

III.

But Time has mowed with the mowers,
　　The boys have boys of their own,
A monster prowls in the meadow,

The daisies of girls are grown,
  I linger and think alone.

IV.

That maple Bethel of summer!—
  I think of its emerald crown,
Whence fell the dapples of shadow,
  Rosettes and a golden brown,
As if a beautiful leopard
  In a timothy lair lay down.

V.

There heroes sit in the noonings
  And gaze on the battle-ground,
And wipe their brows with their jackets,
  And luncheon and laugh go round,
And lads in the yarn suspenders,
  The X-backed boys abound!

VI.

A jug as sleek as a cricket
  Is drawn from a grassy drift,
Swung lightly out by the shoulder,
  Swung up with a dexterous lift,
  Swung back to the bird's-nest rift!

VII.

The mowers all rallied and ready
   Strike in at the leader's word,
Right on through clusters of lilies,
   Those duplicate texts of the Lord,
   And put the broad field to sword!

THE X-BACKED BOYS.

VIII.

The woods grow fine in the distance,
   As moss in a painted urn,
The lady elms and the beeches
   Are patterns in lace that turn
   Asparagus plumes and fern.

IX.

The hills are polished as porcelain
    And tinted with mountain blue,
One lamb-like cloud, as if angels,
    With nought upon earth to do,
    Had brought up by hand a ewe,

X.

Lies clean and white in the welkin
    As snow on a blue-grass hill;
A red-capped drummer is beating
    Tattoo with an ivory bill;
A small brown fifer is playing
    A low and a lazy trill;
    And the blade of a narrow rill
Slips out from under a shadow,
    A scabbard so strangely still,
That what was pictured by willow
    Might well have been cast by hill!

XI.

The birds trail wings in the sunshine
    And sit in a silent row,
The locusts are winding their watches,

THE MOWERS.

The butterflies opening slow,
Like flame are the flowers in blow.

XII.

A breeze drops out of the maple
And travels the rippling grain,
The fog lifts white from the river,
The glorified ghost of rain
Ascending to Heaven again.

XIII.

The fields are grand in their velvet,
The tall grass rustles red,
The bees boil up in their anger,
The meadow-lark leaves her bed,
Right onward the mowers tread!

XIV.

With steady stride they are swaying
The snath with the chronic writhe,
A wispy rush and a rustle,
A swing to the grasses lithe,
Right home through the swath the scythe!

XV.

Then rising, falling, and drifting,
    As buoys on the billows ride,
The braided brims of the shadows
    Afloat on the red-top tide
    The brows of the mowers hide.

XVI.

The blades are rasping and sweeping,
    The timothy tumbles free,
The field is ridgy and rolling
    With swaths like the surging sea
    Heaped up to the toiler's knee.

XVII.

Hark! *whit-to-whit* of the whetstone,
    The stridulous kiss of steel,
The shout of winners exultant
    That distance the field and wheel
    As gay as a Highland reel.

XVIII.

Swing right! Swing left! And the mowers
    Stream out in a sea-bird flight.

The line grows dimmer and dotted
   With flickering shirt-sleeves white
   Washed clean in the morning light.

XIX.

The steel-cold eddies are whirling
   About and about their feet,
Die, Clover, Grasses and Daisies!
   No dead in the world so sweet,
   Ye Slain of the windrow street!

XX.

Oh, wreck and raid of September!
   Oh, prodigal death to die!
'Til April gay with her ribbon,
   Comes bringing the blue-bird sky,
   Oh, lilies of Christ, good-by!

LIFE ON THE FARM.

MILKING TIME.

A T the foot of the hill the milk-house stands,
Where the Balm of Gilead spreads his hands,
And the willow trails at each pendent tip
The lazy lash of a golden whip,
And an ice-cold spring with a tinkling sound
Makes a bright green edge for the dark green ground.

Cool as a cave is the air within,
Brave are the shelves with the burnished tin
Of the curving shores, and the seas of white
That turn to gold in a single night,
As if the disc of a winter noon
Should take the tint of a new doubloon!

Burned to a coal is the amber day.
Noon's splendid fire has faded away,
And, lodged on the edge of a world grass-grown,

Like a great live ember, glows the sun;—
When it falls behind the crimson bars
Look out for the sparks of the early stars.

With the clang of her bell a motherly brown —
No trace of her lineage handed down —
Is leading the long deliberate line
Of the Devons red and the Durhams fine.
"Co-boss!" "Co-boss!" and the caravan
With a dowager swing comes down the lane,
And lowing along from the clover bed
Troops over the bars with a lumbering tread.

Under the lee of the patient beasts,
On their tripod stools like Pythian priests,
The tow-clad boys and the linsey girls
Make the cows "give down" in milky swirls.
There's a stormy time in the drifted pails,
There's a sea-foam swath in the driving gales,
Then girls and boys with whistle and song,
Two pails apiece, meander along
The winding path in the golden gloom,
And "set" the milk in the twilight room.

NIGHT ON THE FARM.

Now all clucked home to their feather beds
Are the velvety chicks of the downy heads,
In the old Dutch style with the beds above,
All under the wings of a hovering love,
But a few chinked in, as plump as wrens,
Around the edge of the ruffled hens!

With nose in the grass the dog keeps guard,
With long-drawn breaths in the old farm-yard
The cattle strand on the scattered straw,
And cease the swing of the under jaw.

The cat's eyes shine in the currant bush,
Dews in the grass and stars in the hush,
And over the marsh the lightning-bug
Is swinging his lamp to the bull-frog's chug,
And the slender chaps in the greenish tights,
That jingle and trill the sleigh-bells nights.
The shapes with the padded feet prowl round
And the crescent moon has run aground,
And the inky beetles blot the night
And have blundered out the candle-light!

And everywhere the pillows fair
Are printed with heads of tumbled hair.
Time walks the house with a clock-tick tread,
Without and within the farm's abed!

THE MORNING.

APPRENTICED angels everywhere
Were out all night in the darkened air,
A dome to build and a wall to lay
And shelter the world from outer day.

They smoothed the arch with trowels of night,
Work as they would it never shed light;
They mended the roof with might and main,
But it leaked like broken thatch in the rain.

At crevice and chink the curves of blue
Would let the glory glimmering through
From the countless stars like silver sand
All sifted and sowed with radiant hand.

To show Creation's grain in the sky
God quarried the worlds and let them lie!

That Eastern wall with its granite crown
In the early dawn came tumbling down,
With no more crash than the roses make
When out of the buds the beauties break.

The world is a-fire with a pearl surprise,
A garden gate to our wondering eyes
Is opening into Paradise!
The dews are off and the bees abroad,
The Sun stands armed in the gates of GOD!

THE CHURNING.

No graceful shape like a Grecian urn,
But upright, downright, stands the churn.
Broad at the base and tapering small,
Above it the dasher straight and tall —
Windowless tower with flag-staff bare,
Warrior or warden, nobody there!
Fashioned of cedar, queen of the wood,
Cedar as sweet as a girl in a hood
Hiding her face like a blush-rose bud.

The dasher waits knee-deep in the cream,
As cattle wade in the shady stream,

And flat in the foot as a four-leafed clover,
Just waits a touch to trample it over.

Beside the churn a maiden stands,
Nimble and naked her arms and hands —
Another Ruth when the reapers reap,—
Her dress, as limp as a flag asleep,
Is faced in front with a puzzling check;
Her feet are bare as her sun-browned neck;
Her hair rays out like a lady fern.
With a single hand she starts the churn,
The play at the first is free and swift,
Then she gives both hands to the plunge and lift:

A short quick splash in the Milky Way —
One-two, one-two, in Iambic play —
A one-legg'd dance in a wooden clog,
Dancing a jig in a watery bog —
A soberer gait at an all-day jog —
Up-down, up-down, like a pony's feet,
A steady trot in a sloppy street.
The spattering dash and the tinkling wash
Deaden and dull to a creamy swash —
Color of daffodil shows in the churn!
Glimpses of gold! Beginning to turn!

"BESIDE THE CHURN A MAIDEN STANDS,
NIMBLE AND NAKED HER ARMS AND HANDS."

Slower — and lower — deader and dumb —
Daisies and Buttercups!   Butter has come!

What thinks the maiden all the while?
Whatever she thinks, it makes her smile,
Whatever she does it is only seeming,
Spinning and weaving, wedding and dreaming;
Ah, charms are hid in the ingots gold,
And more come out than the churn can hold!
Not butter at all, but bonnets sown
With gardens of flowers and all full blown;
A clouded comb of the tortoise shell,
Ah, it is a beauty and she a belle!

A grape-leaf breast-pin's restless shine
Is twinkling up from the fairy mine.
The dasher clinks on a bright gold ring,
Morocco shoes, like a martin's wing,
Come up with a gown of flounces silk
Some fairy lost in the buttermilk!
Ribbons of blue for love-knot ties
To match the tint of her longing eyes;—
Ribbons of pink and a belt of gray
Rippling along in a watery way.

She looks at herself in Fancy's glass,

And she sees her own lithe figure pass —

She closes her eyes and looks again,

And sees, as she dreams, the prince of men —

She closes her eyes, and, side by side,

He is the bridegroom and she the bride!

Ah, never, my girl, will visions burn

As bright as rose in the cedar churn!

Ah, what have we won if this be lost:

THE BLESSING FREE AND THE BLISS AT COST!

THE OLD SCHOOL-HOUSE.

LOW-BROWED school-house, silver-sided,
    Crowns Life's Eastern shore,
  Where the downy day-times glided,
  Ere the throngs around the door,
By the Jordan were divided
    Evermore!

Evermore till comes the Master
    Through the gates ajar,
And each faded earthly aster
    Shall have blossomed out a star —
God the Master of *our* master,
    From afar!

Slow the battered door is giving,
    As it gave of yore —
Lo, the life it has been living
    Curved upon the entry floor —

Closed at last on every grieving,

Locked at last with spiders' reeving —

　　Weary door!

Cenotaph of vanished faces

　　Lettered by the dead —

Carved and graved the empty places,

　　Names unmeaning and unsaid,

And no token of the graces

　　That have fled!

As the door of ceaseless swinging,

　　Wander as it will,

Ever to the portal clinging

　　Sweeps its arc and bides there still,

So life's curve is homeward bringing,

So my heart forever winging,

　　Bides there still!

SCHOOL "CALLED."

Don't you hear the children coming,

　　Coming into school?

Don't you hear the master drumming

　　On the window with his rule?

Master drumming, children coming
  Into school?

Tip-toed figures reach the catch,
Tiny fingers click the latch,
Curly-headed girls throng in
Lily-free from toil and sin;

"TIP-TOED FIGURES REACH THE CATCH."

Breezy boys bolt in together,
Bringing breaths of winter weather,—
Bringing baskets Indian-checked,
Dinners in them sadly wrecked:

Ruddy-handed, mittens off,

Soldiers from the Malakoff—

Built of snow all marble white,

Bastions shining in the light,

Marked with many a dint and dot

Of the ice-cold cannon shot!

Hear the last assaulting shout,

See the gunners rally out,

Charge upon the battered door,

School is called, and battle o'er!

SCHOOL TIME.

DON'T you hear the scholars thrumming?

Bumble-bees in June!

All the leaves together thumbing,

Like singers hunting for a tune?

Master mending pens, and humming

Bonny Doon?

As he thinks, a perished maiden

Fords the brook of song,

Comes to him so heavy laden,

Stepping on the notes along,

Stands beside him, blessed maiden!
   Waited long!

Cherry-ripe the glowing stove,
Grammar class inflecting "love,"
" I love — you love, and love we all "—
Bounding States the Humboldts small,
Chanting slow in common time,
Broken China's rugged rhyme:
" Yang-tse-kiang — Ho-ang-ho —"
Heavenly rivers! How they flow!
" Dnieper-Dniester "— Russian snow!

Writing class with heads one way —
Tongues all out for a holiday!
Hark, the goose-quill's spattering grate,
Rasping like an awkward skate,
Swinging round in mighty Bs,
Lazy Xs, crazy Zs —

Here a scholar, looking solemn,
Blunders up a crooked column,—
Pisa's own Italic tower,
Done in slate in half an hour,
Figures piled in mighty sum,
He wets a finger, down they come!

Learners in the Rule of Three,
"I love you, but he loves me!"
Blue eyes, black eyes, gray eyes, three.

Aproned urchin, aged five,
Youngest in the humming hive,
Standing by the Master's knee,
Calls the roll of A, B, C;
Frightened hair all blown about,
Buttered lips in half a pout,
Knuckle boring out an eye,
Saying "P" and thinking "pie,"
Feeling for a speckled bean,
'Twixt each breath a dumb ravine,—
Like clock unwound, but going yet,
He slowly ticks the alphabet:
"A-*ah* — B-*ah* — C-*ah* — D,"
Finds the bean and calls for "E!"

See that crevice in the floor —
Slender line from desk to door,
First Meridian of the school,
Which all the scholars toe by rule.
Ranged along in rigid row,
Inky, golden, brown and tow,

"HER FINGERS DOVE-TAILED, LIPS APART,
STANDS WITH HEAD OF TREMBLING GOLD."

Are heads of spellers high and low,
Like notes in music sweet as June,
Dotting off a dancing tune.

Boy of Bashan takes the lead,—
Roughly thatched his bullet head;—
At the foot an eight-year-old,
Stands with head of trembling gold;
Watch her when the word is missed!
Her eyes are like an amethyst,
Her fingers dove-tailed, lips apart,
She knows that very word by heart!
Swinging like a pendulum,
Trembling lest it fail to come.
Runs the word along the line
Like the running of a vine,
Blossoms out from lip to lip —
Till the girl in azure slip,
Catches breath and spells the word,
Flits up the class like any bird,
Cheeks in bloom with honest blood,
And proudly stands where Bashan stood!

Evening reddens on the wall —
"Attention!"   Now —"Obeisance" all!

The girls' short dresses touch the floor
They drop their curt'sies at the door;
The boys jerk bows with jack-knife springs,
And out of doors they all take wings!

Sparkling smiles along the line,
Beads upon the amber wine,
Sunshine on the river Rhine.
Broken line and clouded wine,
Night upon the river Rhine!
Vanished all — all change is death;
Life is not the counted breath.
The slanting sun low in the West,
Brings to the Master blessed rest.
See where it bridges afternoon,
And slopes the golden day-time down,
As if to him at last was given,
An easy grade to restful Heaven!
His hair is silver — not with light,
His heart is heavy — not with night,
Dying day the world has kissed,
Good-night, Sweethearts! The school's dismissed!

GOING TO SPELLING SCHOOL.

THE broad of a silvery noon!
And the world lies under the moon,
    Under the moon and the snow;
The moon comes out from under a cloud
    And shines on the world below —
The snow, cold white as a linen shroud
    Put on but an hour ago,
Is a pearly web with a silver thread,
Robe for a bridal and not for the dead.

The river is silent as light,
The road is a ribbon of white,
    Ribbon of silk from Japan —
Its borders rich with satin and shine,
    Betray where the sleigh-shoes ran
That iron the snow to a fabric fine,
    And edged like a lady's fan.
Ah, the night is fair as a marble girl,
Dusty with stars and the mother of pearl!

The school-house is red and aloof,
And rolls from its mossy old roof

"THEY LAUGH AND THEY LEAP TO THE GROUND."

Columns of glorified gloom,
As if there grew from the chimney rude
A Smoke-tree clad in its bloom,
A phœnix fair of the burning wood,
Just sprung from the summer room.
With that only trace of an earthly taint
Picture as white as the soul of a saint!

A twanging and trilling of wires!
Are angels attuning their lyres,
Tuning with negligent hand?
Hark, chimes of bells from over the hills
Dance merrily through the land —
The tinkling troll of a hundred rills!
Cymbals of brass from a band!
'Tis the ringing strings of the bells in bronze
Sprinkling the night with their showery tones.

A spell is abroad and a song,
The spellers and singers along,
Wizards and witches by pairs;
In cutters snug are the Adams and Eves,
Eden's own children and heirs!
Bells in the woods, in lieu of the leaves
And bells that the echo wears —

It is *ring, ring, ring*, to the swinging gait,
Then the teams break trot, for the hour is late,
At a *ting-a-ling, ting-a-ling*, galloping rate!

Now over the ridges they ride,
And down through the valley they glide,
    Bring up at the school-house door,
With bundled girls in the quilted hood,
    Edging of down, as of yore,
Their hearts as sweet as the cedar wood,
    Gowns without gusset or gore,
    Vandykes with a peak before,
And their hair glossed down like a blackbird's wings,
And their shoes laced up, and with leather strings!

They laugh and they leap to the ground,
In woolen, all mittened and gowned,
    Lit up with a ribbon blue,
A breath of cloves or of sassafras,
    And innocent eyes so true
That look you back like a looking-glass,
    And cheeks with the roses through,—
All the girls like flowers that are newly blown,
In the zoneless grace of their " London brown,"

Not a charm in bonds, nor a beauty laced,
The cestus of Venus would girdle the waist.

A chorusing crew comes last
In the Family Ark of the past,
    Packing it full and in pairs —
The rude old sleigh, so roomy and red,
    Kitchens not robbed of their chairs,
But strewn with straw like Poverty's bed,
    Millennial lambs in their lairs!
Like an emigrant ship is the lumbering craft,
Crowded and laden both forward and aft,
With a wooden heart surmounting the stern,
Where the teamsters old gave the reins a turn —
Ah, the hearts that throbbed with their youthful blood
Were as free from care as the sculptured wood!

Oh, sweetheart of Visions below,
Old Covenant Ark of the snow,
    Freighted for church at the door!
Two, side by side, on the sheep-skin seat,
    Are bound for Canaan's shore,
The square foot-stove is under their feet,
    A buffalo robe before —

In the two flag chairs that are side by side,
Are the gray old man and his silver bride;—
Still she carries one for the added ten,
May follow the rule and carry again!
Then the boys and girls in their Sunday clothes,
And the rank slopes down as it farther goes,
To three in a row, for the last are least,
Like the sparks of stars in the early East!
Ah, the old red sleigh, be it ever blest!
It has borne the dead to their silent rest,
The bearers, by twos, as they rode abreast —
Has carried the brides, their bedding and "things,"
When the girls were queens and the bridegrooms kings,
To the splay-foot jog of the olden time,
And the *clang, clang, clang,* of the sleigh-bells' chime.

Ah, necklace of melody old,
With apples and walnuts of gold
   That danced to the horses' feet!
The mother bell in the middle hung,
   As big as a "Golden Sweet,"
Then small each way till the string was strung,
   And two filbert bells did meet,
   And two rhyming hearts did beat.

Ah, the beaded bells of the satin street

That beat the air with their tuneful sleet!

Ah, the string is dumb, and as green with rust

As the dimpled graves of the maidens' dust!

DREAMING.

THE HEROES AND THE FLOWERS.

IN Rose Hill, Chicago, stands a monument to the Boys in Blue. It is the Angel Hope, waked by a master from her sleep in the pale tombs of Carrara. A star is over her head, and one hand is lifted toward it as if she had just plucked it fresh from Heaven, or as if she had halted it that it might shine there forever. She keeps watch and ward over the dead soldiers of Bridges' Battery lying at her feet. Their graves radiate from the base of the monument like the rays that encircle the head of the Madonna.

Standing by the Angel one day in May, and looking down upon those beds of peace, whose occupants I had known, and some of whom I had seen in the grand anger of battle, this was the thought: will nothing wake these cannoneers?

Let us try bugles, and they shall not wake them.

Let the drums beat to arms, but they shall not heed them.

We will wheel out the battery and give the thunder-gusts of battle, and they shall slumber right on.

They are hopelessly dead. They are utterly dumb. We must summon witnesses to testify for them who cannot speak, and among them this marble Angel that came all the way across the sea for their sake. That star above her brow is a star fallen out of the Flag! The Flag? And we never thought of it when we would wake the sleepers! Ah, that's the thing. Over all "the pomp and circumstance" of war, over all constitutions and laws, they will surely heed the Flag, and they do, and the dead soldiers answer the roll-call. So, the poem did not blossom like a flower in a week, but opened like a fan in an instant, and who wonders?

That golden day in May, on the threshold of June, the murmur of the distant city, the hush of the multitude, the air sweet with ten thousand flowers, the marble doors of the enduring houses the grave-digger builds, standing far and near, white and still in the sunshine — doors that shall open to mortal love and longing never more — ah, me, I can never forget it, for I shall never look upon its like again.

THE HEROES AND THE FLOWERS.

ROSE HILL.

I.

OH, be dumb all ye clouds
　　As the dead in their shrouds,
　　Let your pulses of thunder die softly away,
Ye have nothing to do
But to drift round the blue,
For the emerald world grants a furlough to-day!

II.

Bud, blossom, and flower,
　　All blended in shower,
In the grandest and gentlest of rains shall be shed
　　On the acres of God
　　With their billows of sod
Breaking breathless and beautiful over the dead!

III.

They do flush the broad land
With the flower-laden hand,
Drift the dimples of graves with the colors of even;
Where a Boy in Blue dreams,
A "Forget-me-not" gleams —
No rain half so sweet ever fell out of Heaven!

IV.

From no angel was caught
The magnificent thought
To pluck daisies and roses, those *bravest* of things,—
For they stand all the while
In their *graves* with a smile —
And to strew with live fragrance dead lions and kings!

V.

It was somebody born,
It was Rachel forlorn,
'Twas the love they named Mary, the trust they called Ruth;
'Twas a *woman* who told
That the blossoms unfold
A defiance to death and a challenge for truth;
That the violet's eye,

Though it sleep, by and by
Shall watch out the long age in the splendor of youth.

VI.

Ah, she hallowed the hour
When she gathered the flower;
When she said, " This shall emblem the fame of my brave ! "
When she thought, " This shall borrow
" Brighter azure to-morrow ; "
When she laid it to-day on the crest of a grave.

———

A great mart's majestic arterial beat
Throbbed this multitude out, where the graves at our feet
Have so roughened the earth with their motionless surge
That we know we are treading its uttermost verge,
That another step more and life's flag would be furled,
Another step more we are out of the world!

Did ye think we had come to give greeting to June,
Who had opened her gates by a May-day too soon,
Breathed her buds into blossom, her birds into song,
And reached here before us by ever so long?
Stay, reverent feet! Bid the bosom be still!
The campaigning is ended — we halt at Rose Hill.

We are looking for comrades off duty forever!
Do you dream that a handful of ashes can sever
The stout sterling hearts that were beating as one,
And kept time as they beat, to the throb of a gun?

Now summon the sexton, master-builder for man,
Who has worked for the world since its dying began —
Bid him tell if he thinks he ever has crushed
Out the love of a heart that was worth the poor dust
That would hide it. I solemnly tell you, no clod
Tolls the knell of the love as immortal as God,
That is born out of danger and christened with blood;
That can look in the graves of dead valor and say
It was grander than living, that passing away,
For they halted the world for the truth and the right,
Said " Begone, mighty Death, and forever good-night! "
And, shoulder to shoulder, let Batteries tell
How they marched within hail of the borders of hell.

Ah, the brave cannoneers overtaken at last!
Here they went into camp when "the dead line" was passed,
Left the turbulent world with a cadence sublime,
And these born sons of thunder had marched out of time,
Worn away for grand orders their glorious scars,
Here they lie, side by side, front face to the stars!

"HERE THEY WENT INTO CAMP
WHEN THE 'DEAD LINE' WAS PASSED."

And I knew we should find them! As ever their wont,

Bridges' Battery Boys always breasted the brunt,

As in life, so in death, they had gone to the "front!"

Will they sleep out their furlough? Blow bugles amain!

Give the old warble breath! Let them hear it again

As they heard it that day when Cumberland's crags

Right up to the sky were a-flutter with flags,

As if eyries of eagles should burst on the sight,

And sweep up the mountain on pinions of might

To meet the gray morning half way in its flight!

Let the sounding recall mock Euroclydon's lips

When it strews the Levant with a million of ships,

And the shout through the roar of the seas as they whelm,

Is "All hands upon deck and two at the helm!"

Oh, ye trumpets give o'er! If the sleepers can hear

They will answer you back with an old-fashioned cheer.

There's a goldfinch aloft on a billow of song,

There's the drift of a leaf as it rustles along—

Can nothing bring utterance out of the sod

But the blast of that angel, the Bugler of God?

Bring out the drum-majors! Strike with ague the air,

Bid them sling up the parchment, and tighten the snare,

While the drums of the drummer-boys beat "the long roll,"

And the surges of thunder rumble up to the pole,

Till they jar the dead clod, till they thrill the live soul.

Stormy pulses be dumb! All unheeded, unheard,

As the heart-beat that troubles the breast of a bird.

Wheel the Battery out! Unlimber the guns!

All flashing electric the eyes of its sons,

All glowing the forges, all ready to fire,

The cannon all panting with keenest desire,

The columns all grander and broader and nigher,

For the souls within range, God pardon their sins!

Let all go, Mighty Heart! and the battle begins.

Each throb is the thunder — a bolt for each flash

Rends the air with a howl, smites the earth with a crash,

And the shriek of the shell with the quivering cry

That a demon might utter if demons could die,

Cuts keen through the din like a wing through the sky;—

Till old Kennesaw roars from its mantle of cloud,

And Lookout stands white before God in its shroud,

As if Gabriel's trumpet had sounded that day,

And the mountain had heard and was first to obey!

And the breath of the battery dims the broad noon,

And the heart of the battery quickens its tune,

It is "Stand by the guns!" It is "Right about wheel!"

It is "In with the iron!" It is "Out with the steel!"

As a squadron swoops down with a roar on the flank —

And it reddens the Ridge and it riddles the rank —

It is God and dry powder forever we thank!

Round the turbulent land its sledges have swung,

In a score of grand battles its melody rung,

Atlanta and Franklin have heard its grand chime,

And before Mission Ridge it gave them the time.

Chickamauga's dread Sunday it thundered "amen"

'Mid the gusts of wild fire, when the iron clad rain

Did ripen brown earth to the reddest of stars,

And baptized it anew and christened it Mars.

In that moment supreme, to their bridles in blood,

Like a rock in the wilderness grandly *he* stood

Till the Red Sea was cleft and he rode down the street,

With the fame on his brow and the foe at his feet!

Oh, be muffled ye drums! Let artillery toll!

Cloud up, all ye flags! Earth has lost a great soul.

Gallant THOMAS, good-night, but good-morn to thy glory,

Outranking them all in the charm of thy story!

Like a shadow in sunshine they have borne thee in state

Far across the new world, to the true "Golden Gate" —

Philip Sydney, make room, for thy comrade is late!

Spike the guns! When their tongues of eloquent fire
Sent the crashing old anthem, that ought to inspire
The pale dead in their graves, around the green world,
Not a cheer fluttered up, not a shroud was unfurled.
Did the men of Chaldea, lone watching afar,
Ever hear, in their dreaming, the throb of a star?
Inarticulate earth! Is there nothing can reach
To thy chambers serene? Can unlock the dead speech?

We have come into court, this court of the Lord,
To bear witness for them who can utter no word.
Bare-hearted, bare-browed, in this presence we stand,
For the gift Pentecostal comes down on the land;
To speak for the speechless how witnesses throng,
And the earth is all voice, and the air is all song!
There's a fleet of white ships blown abroad on the deep,
And their courses forever they peacefully keep,
And they toss us a roar and it melts into words,
And they strike to the heart like the sweeping of swords:
"Would ye honor the men you must look in their graves,
Who did score danger out with their wakes from the waves."

There are soft, fleecy clouds fast asleep in the sun,
Like a flock of white sheep when the washing is done,

Not a breath of a battle is staining the blue,

It is nothing but Paradise all the way through!

There are domes of white blossoms where swelled the white tent,

There are plows in the field where the war-wagons went,

There are songs where they lifted up Rachel's lament.

Would you know what this mighty beatitude cost,

You must search in the graves for what Liberty lost!

Has man waited too long that the silence is broken

By beings that God never meant should have spoken

And that never were born — poor inanimate things

All endowed with the accents of creatures and kings?

Oh, ye living, make way!   For direct from the tomb

Of Carrara a wonderful witness has come —

As fair as an angel, as free from all sin,

With one whisper from God would her pulses begin!

She had lain there forever in marble repose

But Love spoke the word, she grew human, and rose,

At the touch of the sculptor, awoke from the swoon,

Cast off the cold shroud and stood up in the noon!

Will you see where that hand, pure and pale as a drift,

Has just halted a star with its eloquent lift,

That the heroes who lie in their slumber together

May have it for emblem, whatever the weather?

'Tis a spark from the Flag!   Dare ye think they are dead

Without whom the brave star had forever been shed,

And the autumn come down like the night on the world

And our fragment of heaven disaster'd and furled!

Aye! up with the banner and down with the thought!

Fling the "old glory" out till the breezes have wrought

Into billows of beauty its marvelous flame

That can kindle a soul to the color of fame!

Now, Sergeant, the roll! Soft and low, sweet and clear,

The dread silence is cleft, and the answer is "HERE!"

"Here!" Bishop and Seborn! Brave lieutenants, stand fast!

Thanks to God for the flag, we have found you at last!

"Here!" Ferris and Smith! "Here!" Hammond and Brown!

Ye that trod the acanthus and trampled it down,

And it turned at the touch a Corinthian crown.

Here! glorious Score! On our hearts and our lips,

Not a name of ye all can be quenched in eclipse!

Disenthralled from your graves you have left them alone,

We will borrow them now for these dead of our own!

Let us bury all bitterness, passion, and pride,

Lay the rankling old wrong to its rest by their side,

Keeping step to the manhood that marches the zone,

And believe the good GOD will take care of His own!

LAST YEAR'S STARS.

I.

WHEN Science grasped a filmy thread of light
That dimly floated in the empty air,
And dared to draw the silver woof of night
Until she saw a *star* was clinging there,
She trembled at the vision she had seen,
It only told her that a star had been!

II.

That starry tress had faded in its flight,
So long it wandered through the blue abyss,
Before it met a mortal's startled sight.
While yet it journeyed from that world to this,
Perhaps some hand had borne the wondrous urn
Beyond the range of human thought's return,
Perhaps extinguished — e'en the stars do die —
Ere Heaven unfolded to her earnest eye.

III.

Things are around us that have ceased to be,
 And starry hopes, extinguished long ago,
Still link us to the past. Who would be free,
 Or give that tearful past for all we know,
Or dream, of bliss and blessing yet to come?
All, all is mortal till it reach the tomb,
 And all unblest until it find its wings!
That last year's Heaven of stars! Ah, who would give
 For aught besides? Filled with translated things,
Too bright to die, too beautiful to live.

TO MY WIFE.

THERE are thousands who need not stray out of their own hearts to find the reason for recording here this tribute of long ago. The world is full of little graves, and the thousands I mean, have been crowned, each in her tearful turn, the mother of a sinless angel child.

As of the woodman's work, so of the mother's love; it will always be true that the little chips are nearest the heart.

TO MY WIFE.

I.

LUCY, don't you hear the voices, gentle voices in the air;
Like the waving of a pinion, like the panting of a prayer,
Like a song of singers dead,
Like a dream of beauty fled,
When we cannot quite remember what the angel vision said?

II.

Oh, the voices of the Yesterdays! Time's melancholy choir,
With the twilight singing minor and the dawning singing air,
With the clouds of glory round
And their brows with garlands bound,
And a million golden minutes strown like grain upon the ground.

III.

Ah, they must be up the River, and it cannot be a dream,
For the wind is blowing soft, my Love, is blowing *down* the
stream,

And is wafting to your ears

What your list'ning spirit hears,

Till the past grows dim and dimmer through the mist of many
tears.

IV.

And a little form in white seems to rise beyond the rain,

And a little hand to beckon and a little voice complain,

To your heart a moment pressed,

Then away to be a guest,

And to sing among the Angels in the Gardens of the Blest.

V.

For the little infant spirit that a brighter angel bore,

A darker angel challenged at the threshold of the door,

And he bade it back again,

As returns the morning rain

To the heaven o'er the mountain and the glory o'er the main.

VI.

In his arms the angel clasped her, and as he turned and smiled

He crowned you there, the mother of a sinless angel child.

Ah, the beauty that she wore,

Borne so swiftly on before,

Just to learn the Heaven for "welcome" to that bright and
blessed shore!

"AND A LITTLE FORM IN WHITE
SEEMS TO RISE BEYOND THE RAIN."

VII.

But Lucy, 'twill be by and by, when Junes have followed June,
And many a sad December night has played a solemn tune;
　　When the snow upon your hair
　　Forgets to melt and lingers there,
And a form so frail and faded trembles in the old arm-chair.

VIII.

Then here's my hand, my Dearest, we'll travel on together,
In days both clear and cloudy, in rude and rainy weather,
　　Till the winter at the last
　　Shall the shadows Eastward cast,
And our lives and loves forever shall be blended with the Past.

MONUMENTS.

ALAS, for the land where "God's acres" are vain,
    And the heroes grow grass and not heroes again,
    And Valor and Virtue wronged out of the grace
That can make of the grave a most eloquent place.
They have melted dumb guns, and the effigies start
Like the Worthies of old from the furnace's heart.
They have knocked at the ledge of white limestone, and said:
"Oh, ye sleepers, awake! and come forth, oh ye dead!"
And, the stone from the sepulchre lifted away,
The pale marble immortals stand up in the day!
The untenanted tombs tumble in at their feet,
And beside them two centuries mingle and meet.

MISSION OF SONG.

I.

HOW beautiful and strange! The air that brings
  The sweet small gospel from the broider'd sod,
  Through which we see the starry camps of Even—
  Stained through and through with glory and with
   Heaven—
That floats the cloudy squadrons of a God,
  Breaks into billows when a sparrow sings,
  And lends these lives of ours immortal wings!

II.

 Those bird-like breaths of song sweep o'er the dumb,
Where waves the corn on old red fields of fame:
  We call the roll: in accents loud and clear,
  Along the lines the soldiers answer "Here!"
And each green billow renders up a name—
  With ranks unbroken, lo the columns come,
  And old dead captains march at beat of drum!

III.

Though David's crown is only rust,
Yet the stately step of his royal Psalms
    Is as fresh as May in the fragrant dust,
And grand as the wind in the Palms.
        'Tis a bird in the sky!
        'Tis an Archangel nigh!
The whisper of God in the calms!

    Corunna's Hero walks the world
With the rhythmic march of his Burial Song —
    With bugle wail and banner furled
The old dead troopers ride along,
        And Marion's men
        Start out of the glen
With their cheer so wild and strong.

    Hark! Korner's Sword Song rings amain,
With its wild "hurrah" for his iron bride —
    Bozzaris strikes for the Greeks again,
And the Light Brigade will ride
        Through the Valley of Death,
        At the Poet's breath,
And fall into rank by our side!

IV.

A Child of Song lay dying, and his breath
Went sad and slow as moves the March in Saul;
　　His hands were folded white upon his breast,
　　Like two sweet doves that wearied and had rest.
Those hands had touched all hearts and kindled all,
　　Until the songs came forth like birds in Spring 'neath
　　Cottage eaves. If he *could* die, then this was death.

V.

Then came a breath or two of some brave strain
A hand began within another room,
　　And trembled there a poor unended tune,
　　A single dew-drop on the breast of June:
But twilight stained anew that growing gloom —
　　Those hands unfolding swept the chords again,
　　Gave the last note and played the sweet refrain.
　　Oh, Child of Song, how grandly thou didst die,
　　Thy Life's last cadence a melodious sigh!

VI.

These lives of ours have rhythm: every one
A little note of that great Anthem, TIME,

Forever sounding down the world amain

Since fell the hammers swung by Tubal Cain.

How grand the footfall ringing out subliine!

How grand to think that Anthem long begun,

Without *our* music never can be done!

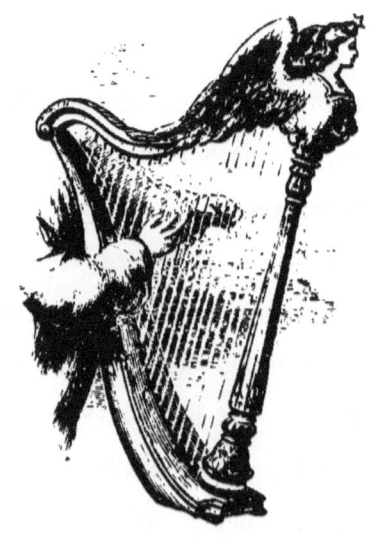